HIS LADY

5 TRAITS OF A GODLY AMBITIOUS WOMAN

Aji R. Michael

Graceful Living

HIS LADY: 5 TRAITS OF A GODLY AMBITIOUS WOMAN

Credits for Book cover image: Forever88 via dreamstime.com

ISBN 978-0-9574219-6-7 (paper edition)
ISBN 978-0-9574219-7-4 (hardcover)

Printed in the United Kingdom

PRAISE FOR 5 TRAITS OF A GODLY AMBITIOUS WOMAN

When I first saw the title: 'His Lady, 5 Traits of a Godly Ambitious Woman', I pondered over the phrase, 'godly ambitious woman'. Am I one? What are the qualities I need to possess in order to qualify as a godly ambitious woman? With those questions running through my mind, I knew I would have to read this book to ascertain if I fell into this category of women, and if I found myself lacking, I would have to work diligently to become a godly ambitious woman, because 'godly ambitious' did not sound bad at all.

While reading this book, I realized that one message echoed through: a godly ambitious woman works hard and pursues greater heights, but "not at any cost." This is the definition of a godly ambitious woman. Aji describes her as a confident lady with desires and strong faith; a prayer warrior; one who does not depend on liquid cash to live a rich life.

I highly recommend this book to every woman, especially those at the start of their careers. You have the chance to start well and get it right. Aji leverages her vast experience and knowledge to help you find your path to success. Will you embrace this chance to save yourself from merry go rounding? I believe it's a yes.

This is a book that will bless you beyond measure. This one will set your thoughts and mind right to go out and be all that God has called you to be as His lady, but not at any cost: not at the detriment of your family, not at your own life's expense and not to the disappointment of your Creator, God.

You most likely have the same questions I had when I first saw the book title. If you do, and you seek answers, then this book is a must-read. And if you are not a godly ambitious woman or you struggle to be one, this book will teach you how to be one.

Feyikemi Oyewole
Founder, Inspirational with Hannah
& Best selling Author of Forgiveness:
Your Access Code

Aji has adeptly used scriptures and sometimes personal stories to share how rightly we can both find our purpose and achieve our ambitions as God's Girls.

This book made me re-embrace ambition knowing that God doesn't disapprove of my wanting to be more, or of wanting to give more.

I hope that everyone who reads this, can both be more and give more.

Nkiru Olumide-Ojo
Executive Head, Regional Marketing &
Communication at Standard Bank
Group South Africa

At the heart of Aji's brilliant and inspiring book is a simple premise: To guide you step by step teaching the secrets of realizing your full potential and stepping outside of the "box" and making breakthroughs.

Shaneen Clarke
Best selling Author
International Speaker

ALSO BY AJI R. MICHAEL

THE NEXT MAVERICK: Ready to shape the future.

LEVERAGE: Proven Strategies To Fulfil
Your Leadership Aspirations

THE PURPOSE-DRIVEN CAREER: 3 breakthrough
steps to find happiness, joy, and fulfillment in your
career no matter your title or company

DREAMS & THOUGHTS JOURNAL

ACKNOWLEDGEMENT

I want to thank my son Alex who has been patient when I stayed up late to work on the book. He put up with my crankiness when I had not gotten enough sleep and he helped with house chores when I needed to catch up on sleep. You have been an amazing son and the dynamics of your growth has taught me what unconditional love is – I love you son! One more book this year we agreed.

I could not have done this without the GRACEFUL LIVING PRAYER TEAM. You ladies have been right there with me every step of the way. Waking up at 5am praying with me and for me is a gift I'll forever adore. I know that even though they will read this book and be encouraged by it, it is more about them pushing me to pursue God in every area of my life.

Thank you, Kemi Oyesola, for being my sounding board, editor, providing clarification on a biblical question or shedding some light on what I was trying to convey. You directed me and guided me through this process, and I appreciate it.

I want to thank my brother, Kunle Arisilejoye, whom

God has placed in my life as my backbone. No one would be able to comprehend the magnitude of my adventurous journey like you. You were there for me when my life was planted like a seed, I was filled with darkness but you kept assuring me there was light. Thank you for leading me to Christ, I still have the book you gave me, which I never opened until five years after – *I Dare To Call Him Father*. Thank You!

Most of all, I want to thank my best friend, adventure partner, Holy Spirit who has been by my side all these years. You have made my Heavenly Father and Jesus so real to me and have been faithful even when I have not been.

CONTENTS

PREFACE

There comes a time in the evolution of every soul when the topmost concern is no longer the survival of the physical body, but the growth of the spirit;

no longer the attainment of worldly success, but the realisation of Self.

In a sense, this is a very dangerous time, particularly at the outset, because the entity housed in the body now knows it is just that: a being in a body not a 'body-being'. At this stage, before the growing entity matures in this point of view, there is often a sense of no longer caring about affairs of the body in any way.

The soul is so excited about being "discovered" at last! The mind abandons the body, and all matters of the body. Everything is ignored. Relationships are set aside.–Family disappears. Jobs are made secondary. Bills go unpaid. The body itself is not even fed for long periods. The entire focus and attention of the entity are now on the soul and matters of the soul. This can lead to a major personal crisis in the day-to-day life of the being.

My Moment of Discovery

In my years of working with women, I've met many smart, hardworking, well-intentioned individuals who are unfulfilled in their spiritual lives. I observed how well they hid their frustrations which in many cases was the source of their many fears, insistent pressure, and constant insecurity.

Many of these women had done lots of personal development work, but were still stressed, stuck in anxiety that held them back from enjoying life and from making more of an effort to use their unique gifts and talents.

These women were some of the greatest, most passionate, and talented people I had ever met, which contributed to how much it bothered me. It just seemed wrong and unfair that such smart, positive, and willing people would struggle so much with life.

It became clear that the common denominator with many of my clients as well as some of my close acquaintances was the struggle and limitation related to doing what they were meant to be doing. And it all boils down to the pressure of wanting to be perceived in a certain way. These women allowed society and circumstances, friends and family to influence who they are and what they should be doing.

This reality drove me to dig deeper and pushed me into writing this book.

A few years ago, I struggled with the same issues; if there's anything that has given me grief in life; it's *"finding my purpose"*.

I grew up in a religious background where I was taught that God is some angry tyrant, and you must appease Him, so you work really hard to avoid his anger. But I wasn't trying to avoid his anger, I wanted to please Him.

I wanted Him to look down from heaven like he did with Job and say, **"Have you seen my daughter, Aji?"**

I wanted God to be proud of me, so I felt I needed to do great things for God; I completed my Masters in Strategy & Change with good grades, went ahead to pursue my MBA, and passed my Executive Coaching Certification with a distinction! But I was nowhere near - the hunger never left.

I endured an abusive marriage for as long as I could, I thought perhaps that'll make God happy.

I allowed friends and family take advantage of me, my resolve - after all, they did it to Jesus!

Every seminar and workshop I attended left me more perplexed. **Oh did I mention that the 6-figure salary didn't tick the box either?**

Let me ask you?

- Do you want to do something big for God, but you feel stuck?

  or

- Do you wonder sometimes what you are supposed to be doing with your life?

I don't know a single Christian who hasn't gotten stressed out over trying to figure out the will of God. We want to solve the mystery of the will of God the way we solve Sudoku or a crossword puzzle. But in my experience, intellectual analysis usually results in spiritual paralysis. We try to make God fit within the confines of our cerebral cortex. We try to reduce the will of God to the logical limits of our left brain. But the will of God is neither logical nor linear. It can be downright confusing and complicated.

A part of us feels as if something is spiritually wrong with us when we experience circumstantial uncertainty. Most of us will have no idea where we are going most of the time. And I know that is unsettling. But circumstantial uncertainty also goes by another term: **adventure.** And nothing is more unnerving or disorienting than passionately pursuing God. The sooner we come to terms with that spiritual reality, the more we will enjoy the journey. I cannot, in good conscience, promise safety or certainty, but I can promise that being ambitious for God's will, will be anything but boring!

"Intellectual Analysis Usually Results In Spiritual Paralysis."

My own adventure started in July 2012 while I was at work, my spirit was really troubled so I went to one of the quiet rooms to pray. I sat there for like five minutes, but I couldn't utter a word. The only words I could pray were *"God I want to do your will; I am ambitious for you."* I cannot recollect how many times I repeated these words which I later turned into a constant prayer (*still do*). That prayer became a seed that got planted in the ground, though it disappeared for a season, it eventually bears fruits. And that's exactly what I'll like to share with you.

"But Circumstantial Uncertainty Also Goes By Another Term: Adventure."

In **HIS LADY**, I want to give you some tools to put in your tool belt that will help you to walk in victory and fullness of life as you embark on your ambitious journey.

In the pages that follow you'll meet some adventurous women. Mind you, they're ordinary women. They have doubts and fears and problems just like you and me. But their courage to come out of the cage and go on an adventure in order to be part of God's bigger picture will inspire and challenge you to follow them as they follow the Holy Spirit's leading.

Let's talk about the godly ambitious woman

If you bought this book, you probably responded on a gut level to the words *'godly ambitious'* in the title. It is a term that describes our primal longing for adventure.

Though the word 'ambition' is an expression that most people react to viscerally because of the negative vibes attached to it, if you watch people who lead organisations, you'll find that they share similar traits: Ambition and Drive. Whether you are a man or a woman, you don't get to the top without these traits. The problem, however, is that while men are admired for these traits, women are often viewed in a negative light, with labels like 'overbearing' and 'un-feminine.' The irony, of course, is that women who lack these traits rarely make it to the top.

We are taught at an early age that ambition is important, but when we witness how society views powerful women, we lose the steam to move up, move forward and move ahead.

I believe to truly shatter the proverbial glass ceiling; we need to start by better defining and modeling ambition for women and girls. We need to ensure that the connotation captures the positives of the concept - "making a difference in the world and being one's best self." Without a positive mindset about ambition, we will continue to see women losing their interest in leadership positions and unable to fulfill their potential to its fullest.

The godly ambitious woman I am writing about is composed of two elements – an open, inquisitive mind and a drive to succeed. Success can be defined in many ways but to her, it's not always about money, and certainly never only about it. She simply knows what she stands for and that motivates her to action. Her motivation for success comes from doing the will of God and for the glory of God. It's an ambition that is anchored in the power of God, the grace of God, and the word of God.

Let's start with the very first trait of a godly ambitious woman.

Trait 1

She is BOLD

So let us come *boldly* to the throne of our
gracious God. There we will receive his
mercy, and we will find grace to help us
when we need it most.

Hebrews 4:16 (NLT)

Chapter 1

Ask, for it is given

I had been success-driven my entire adult life. I got involved in almost every business and network possible and sought to be a leader in each of them. But one issue always hindered me when it came to my choices: I was an extreme people pleaser. I avoided positions that might mean making decisions that would offend people. This was an insecurity I took with me into my marriage and career. I believe I had my fair share of success in business and my career at some point took a quantum leap, but I never did feel at peace. I yearned for more—though I couldn't at that point articulate what the *'more'* was. But I knew I was addicted to success and my emotionally unavailable and financially hazardous ex-husband couldn't have been a better match.

My ex-husband was hardly at home; he was always on business trips funded by me while I still looked after the home affairs. In time, my excessive drive to keep things together became so stressful that it affected my health, and I couldn't tell at that time if I had a marriage or not. The whole race was wearing me out and I became mentally and emotionally immobilised. No amount of money could fix what I was dealing with and my productivity was going down the drain. Suddenly, I wanted to live, not exist.

As I sat down in that quiet room praying, "Lord I want to do your will", I was willing to give every penny if only I could have myself back. My breakdown was the best thing that could have happened for my future. It brought me to a place where I finally submitted myself to His will in all things.

As I stood up to return to my desk, suddenly a scripture lit up my spirit. "Let us come *boldly* to the throne of our gracious God…" I sat back and meditated on this scripture for a while and all the way back home that evening. I later developed a process that allows me to approach God with bold confidence, hear His voice and obey Him — to wait on God for both His timing and His will in my decisions. This process has brought me clarity and complete peace from the Lord and I have never been disappointed by the outcome. Not once.

THE SCENE

The normal rule in Israel, as a patriarchal society, was that inheritances were passed from father to sons. But in the story of Noah and her sisters; Mahlah, Hoglah, Milcah, and Tirzah, something new is instituted. What if a man who died with the older generation in the wilderness had only daughters and no sons?

Who would inherit?

Who would carry on the family name?

Moses takes this case before God, and a new edict is given not only in this particular case, but in general, women without brothers will be able to inherit from their father. The move from the old generation to the new in the wilderness gave rise not only to new life in the Promised Land for all, but to new possibilities for women.

Ask for More

Our opening scene is taken from the Bible in Numbers 27. In this chapter, we discover a special case of inheritance not specifically covered in the Law of Moses: a man named Zelophehad had five daughters, and no sons. Also, inheritance passed from father to son, not from father to daughter. Through no fault of their own, these daughters of Zelophehad were unmarried, fatherless women with no prospect of inheritance rights. How could they live and support themselves in the Promised Land? And even more so, in life as a whole?

What would they do?

The writer to the Hebrews exhorts us to "come boldly to the throne of grace, that we may obtain mercy and find grace to help in time of need" (Hebrews 4:16 KJV). The Greek word translated *boldly* indicates 'freeness of speech, or unreserved expression - all out-spokenness, frankness, bluntness, publicity. As believers, we have the privilege of approaching God freely, without reservation, and without need of long, grandiloquent prayers. We can always have confidence that He always gives us a fair hearing. But we are not always bold when it comes to dealing with external factors - people, culture, religion etc.; we come up with different excuses, an attempt to explain the situation away.

*"As Believers, We Have The Privilege
Of Approaching God Freely, Without
Reservation And Without The Need Of
Long, Grandiloquent Prayers"*

Let's examine some of the external challenges these women had to confront.

Social Traditions

Let us for a moment imagine how this appeal of the daughters of Zelophehad arose. Canaan is now very near, and God has just told Moses the great general principles on which it is to be allotted. Thus, the minds of the people are naturally filled with thoughts of the inheritance. They can no longer complain of being in the wilderness and so Canaan was looked forward to with great expectation.

In such circumstances, every family would be on the look-out with anticipation and assert its share. So here we may well suppose that the sons of Hepher were only too ready to reckon the daughters of their brother Zelophehad as outside any right to the land that would fall to Hepher's children. Natural relations are only too easily trampled on in the greed of gain. Very possibly, the brothers of Zelophehad told their nieces that they had no claim to inherit, it being the settled custom that inheritances were to go to sons.

Let them be satisfied with marriage into some other family. But the daughters felt they also were worthy of an inheritance even though the law was that only men received inheritances and was the norm/tradition/culture, they went ahead to ask with strong reason too – "Our Dad had no sons, so? Why should his name simply disappear just because he had no sons? Give to us a possession too, after all, we are human beings; we do not need to be male to have some of the possession."

Injustice

This was unheard of in that day and age! Women going before the male leadership to question the law of inheritance – it just did not happen. If you look back at Numbers chapter 26, you will see that God called Moses to take a census of the new generation of Israel, who were about to enter the Promised Land. Within this list you will find all the names of the males who were the heads of the tribes, clans and families. The women were not numbered.

So, it required boldness for the five daughters to approach Moses before all the congregation of Israel! In fact, to their merit, the laws of inheritance follow this precedence. From then on, one who died without sons would have his daughters inherit his estate.

Authority

We have imagined an actual refusal to let these women share in the possession. But even if it were not definite; they had a shrewd idea of what will happen, and came appealing to Moses, in the most public manner, so that they may have the weight of his authority to settle the matter. They were women yet had the courage to break away from the conventional rather than tamely submit to injustice.

Mahlah and her sisters approached Moses and the other leaders boldly and with confidence and went straight to the point (another nuance of *boldly* in Hebrews 4:16).

In many ancient cultures, women did not have personal or property rights. Thus, it is noteworthy that Mahlah and her sisters had the confidence, faith, and freedom to approach Moses and Eleazer with their question about their inheritance: *"Why should the name of our father be removed from among his family because he had no son? Give us a possession among our father's brothers"* (Numbers 27:4 NKJV).

Who was to speak for these women, if not they? When the down-trodden find no satisfactory advocate among spectators, it is time for them to raise and use their own voices.

Boldness Has a Voice

If you've been following me on social media, you've probably read or heard me on several occasions share my very interesting story of an abusive marriage. The backstory is that my ex-husband was never violent towards me but I jokingly share with my friends that I wish that was the case as the abusive words were so powerful to the extent that I began to believe and accept some of the words he spoke to me and at me about me.

When you've known someone for years, chances are you want to give their words some thought. I believe that coercion, emotional abuse, and controlling behavior can be just as devastating and is even more difficult for victims to recognise.

His words hunted me so severely that I disengaged from friends, avoided high paying jobs and hardly seized any meaningful opportunity; all because I believed those words and lived them. I did not realise what was happening at first, but then with research and information, the scales fell from my eyes. My deliverance finally came one day when the Holy Spirit inspired me to read Genesis chapter 1, as I read further these words hit me hard; "….and God said…and there was….and it was good."

"... These Words Hit Me Hard; "….and God said… and there was….and it was good."

I would immerse myself in this chapter and other ones; I also pulled out some scriptures to recite all through the day and by the time I'd recouped some boldness, I started confronting him with the 'truth.' For instance: he would say, "You this prostitute!"

theoretically he was right as I've had other relationships before marriage but that wasn't the 'truth.' So, I'll respond stylishly and confidently with a smile, *"Thank you for the reminder, just so you know, it is written if any man* (including a woman-my addition) *be in Christ, he is a new creature, old things have passed away and all things have become new."*

I kept saying these words privately and at countless times when the situation presented itself until I started 'BECOMING' my confession.

You see, all this while, I was already successful, I just didn't own it and obviously didn't feel successful. I later realised that 'the glass ceiling' is a myth and began to expose my own hidden fears and inner barriers that had prevented me from taking full advantage of opportunities.

Do you know of any woman who had the chance to stand up and speak up but never did? Well, I have! The temptations and the pleasures of this world lead them away from the right path and prevent them from having a fair share of their portion.

Like the daughters of Zelophehad, are you bold enough to go on an adventure to have a portion in the Promised Land?

Being BOLD

You don't 'Do' bold. You need to 'Be' bold. Boldness is 'Being'. Being is state, such as 'being happy.' You cannot explain state, nor can you do a state. You can only be a state. You cannot do happiness; you can only be happy. In fact, nothing happens without being.

"...His [God's] Blessing Is Irreversible.
The Lord Has Blessed His People And
He Would Have Them Know It."

Happy conditions do not make you happy. It is **being** happy that causes happy conditions. Unhappy conditions only show up to prove your pre-existing state of unhappiness. Your **being** influences your thinking, that is, who you are (in Christ) determines what you think on, which affects your speaking, which causes doing, which puts in place the system to receive and experience what you created in your **being** and thinking.

Remarkable success in your business and career endeavours is as a result of your being bold and not the other way around as most people do. Your '**Being**' is your source – your identity. After all, you are a human '**Being**.'

"In Fact, Nothing Happens Without Being."

Boldness Powered by Identity

No doubt, wearing beautiful clothes, having a fantastic career and social status are confidence boosters and can in some cases be a source of boldness. But what happens if suddenly, all of those are taken away, you not only lose your boldness but of course, your power too.

Have you ever wondered how the women in our story got the boldness to challenge Moses and the elders? I think it's because they had a sense of the Lord's blessings over their lives and that His blessing is irreversible. The Lord has blessed His people and He would have them know it.

"And the Lord spoke unto Moses, saying, Speak unto Aaron and unto his sons, saying, On this wise you shall bless the children of Israel, saying unto them, The Lord bless thee, and keep thee: the Lord make His face shine upon thee, and be gracious unto thee: the Lord lift up His Countenance upon thee, and give thee peace. And they shall put My name upon the children of Israel; and I will bless them." Numbers 6:22-27(KJV)

Note that Aaron did not bless the people of his own will. He did not utter good words of his own composition but there went forth a Divine power which made the form of blessing to be a blessing indeed. The blessing is sure.

The blessing was not to cease from generation to generation. That blessing fell upon us in the beginning, when we were converted, and it has never ceased! You are forever the blessed of the Lord. He blesses us all today and it is His wish that we should experience the fullness of this blessing. **Do you have a sense of the Lord's blessings?**

"Your Boldness Should Be Rooted In Your True Identity And Not In What You Do Or Have."

Boldness is in your DNA

Everything you need to be beautiful, successful, incredible, blessed, trusted, respected, honored, and happy are already in your life. It may not seem like it, but only because you're focused on the wrong things. Anything birthed prematurely risks complications. The complications you've faced that made you stop being bold are simply things that you gave birth to too soon. Your boldness should be rooted in your true identity and not in what you do or have.

When I think of a Queen, of course, I think of the pomp and circumstance of it all, the beauty and grace with which she must walk through life. Oh, I can imagine the mornings waking up to the beauty of the palace bedroom with all its luxury. I can see in my mind's eye the opulence of the furniture and fixtures. I can see myself being waited on by my lady's maid, getting my bath ready, pressing my clothes, getting my make up on, and having my hair done so that I don't have bad hair days ever again. Then I see myself going over my itinerary for the day and having my driver pick me up to take me to my first very important appointment …

Oh, sorry, I got a little carried away there with daydreaming of being a Queen.

But besides all the luxury and pampering, there are also the practical matters of royal life and the central part of that is her position in the royal family. As a Queen, her lineage is clear. She does not wonder if she is accepted or question her right to be in the family. She does not wake up and wonder if she has been good enough to remain a part of the royal family. She knows that she owns the kingdom and her position in the family is as solid as a rock.

Just as the Queen has a position and she is confident in her **Being**, we can walk in that same boldness. God does not change His mind. He is faithful and trustworthy in His promises. You are a joint heir in the Royal Family. And with that comes the **boldness** to walk with your head held high because you are the King's Lady. Your position in the Kingdom of God is secure. You are **His Lady**.

Take the Holy Spirit out of the equation of my life, and it would spell b-o-r-i-n-g. If you would describe your relationship with God as anything less than adventurous, then maybe you think you're following the Holy Spirit but have settled for something less — something I refer to as 'inverted Christianity'. Instead of following the Holy Spirit, you invite the Holy Spirit to follow you. The result of this inverted relationship with God is not just a self-absorbed spirituality that leaves us feeling empty, it's also the difference between spiritual boredom and spiritual adventure.

I got this message from a client: "*For years the only relationship I had with myself was one of doubt. I doubted my decisions, whether I was saying or doing the right thing…whether I was in any way pleasing God, or anybody else. I knew I wasn't pleased with myself, so how could God or anybody else be pleased with me? Those years of misery are behind me now, I realised I was so bound by legalistic religion that I'll always have to be on guard against it. But now I know how to recognise its symptoms.' Now at any time I can answer the call of God with confidence, knowing that God does not waste anything. He uses every strength, weakness, heartache, success, relationship, and experience to shape our hearts, to draw us closer to him, and to equip us to fulfill our life's calling – His ultimate will.*"

Boldness is Adventure

I love the Church. But too often, I feel we take people out of their natural habitat and try to tame them in the name of religion. We try to remove the risk. We try to remove the danger. We try to remove the struggle. And what we end up with is a caged Christian.

Deep down inside, all of us long for more. Sure, the tamed part of us grows accustomed to the safety of the cage. But the untamed part longs for some danger, some challenge, some adventure. And at some point in our spiritual journey, the safety and predictability of the cage no longer satisfies. We have a primal longing to be uncaged. And the cage opens when we recognize that we are not on this revolving globe to just sit on the boat – the real adventure is walking on water.

Let me ask you a question?

"... Being Bold Makes Your Path Easier."

When was the last time you asked God to bid you 'come' like He did Peter to walk on water - to go on an adventure? I would like to think that by the time you complete this book; you'll leave your natural habitat and boldly go on an adventure spree.

Seize the moment

I wish I'd had the boldness to take certain actions in the early years of my career. I was giving up before I even got started. I know many women with similar talents who positioned themselves lower and lesser simply because they were not bold enough to seize the moment. They underestimated their abilities, so they aimed for less than they were capable of. And that's exactly what they got! Years may pass before they become exasperated from functioning in a place below their desire.

Whether in your relationships, career, financial abilities, health and fitness habits, or spiritual journey, *being* bold makes your path easier.

Warning: Do not confuse Boldness with Brashness

If you're smart and driven, someone whom other people think of as a go-getter, you may be telling yourself right now that you already have the 'Bold' trait. But go-getting is not the same as the 'Boldness' I infer here. Now I'm not trying to dumb down your achievements, but I've seen women share some of theirs with me and when you look at them, they're just taking care of the basics – more like a tick box exercise.

When you bought this book, I don't think it was simply because of the title *HIS LADY*. I suspect the word *'ambition'* captured your fancy. There's a part of you that's ready for change, that wants much more and has begun to suspect you need a bold move in order to get it.

Here are some attributes of *being* bold for you to reflect on:

1. She has a clear goal for the future
2. She trusts her instincts 99% of the time and never worries about people's opinions

3. She doesn't worry whether people like her

4. She doesn't keep a low profile, she walks and talks like a winner

5. She doesn't follow the conventional way of doing things, she creates her own rules

6. She doesn't always wait for opportunities, she creates them

7. She doesn't act like a man, she stands in her feminine power

8. She believes in her capability, as such she doesn't need to lie, cheat, or steal

9. She takes smart risks

10. She doesn't think of only herself, but the greater good of all.

WOMAN WITH
THE ALABASTER OIL

We don't know her name, age or history. We know only that she was bad for a season. To be specific, she sold her body for money. Because her sinful lifestyle was common knowledge, people whispered about her, eyed her with disdain, avoided her company.

This woman showed up at Simon's (one of the Pharisees) house alone bearing a small alabaster flask of perfume. She drew closer, then stood behind him at his feet weeping, she wet his feet with her tears and our bold lady then reached for her alabaster box and poured perfume on his feet.

Jesus then turned toward our repentant chic, even though His host Simon began to doubt in his heart if Jesus was truly a prophet.

*Jesus said: **"Do you see this woman?"** And then He made a pronouncement: "Her sins, which are many, are forgiven."*

Jesus offered the woman a final word of assurance: "Your faith has saved you; go in peace" Luke 7: 50 (NLT) Wow!

Peace? Yes, please. What woman doesn't need more of that in her life?

If you'd have to look beyond your past, what bold move are you prepared to make now?

YOUR GUIDE TO THE FUTURE

Trait 1 – Be BOLD

1. Who Do I want to be? This is the most important question you need to first ask yourself. Write down the trait or traits you want to embody.

2. What actions can I take to become the woman I desire to be? Write them down. If your description of YOU is not BOLD, acknowledge it and do something about it. Speak to someone who loves and knows you about it.

3. Now ask for exactly what you want – in prayer. Be BOLD. Write it down in detail. Do not leave anything out.

4. Now, ask for MORE – everything – that you desire. Be BOLD. Write it down.

5. Who do you need to speak to, so that you can set it in motion? It could be your boss at work, the CEO of your organisation; it could be you need to hire a Coach, speak to your Mentor, etc. DECIDE. Who? Be BOLD and approach that person in the next <u>24 hours</u>. Use your VOICE. Do not write an email or letter or even a message via your phone to this person except to let them know you would like to have a 1:1 meeting with them. If you write, suggest a date and time to meet.

6. Now, go on that 'adventure.' Write out what you

will say at the 1:1 meeting. Be BOLD. Write out EXACTLY what you want to say and the RESULT you want to have at the meeting – the EXACT RESULT. Because this will determine how you posture and position yourself during the meeting and before.

7. Do not accept 'NO' as the final verdict. Knock on another door and keep knocking. You may need to have a series of meetings to get the RESULT you want. Be BOLD.

Trait 2

She has a DESIRE

For God is working in you, giving you the
desire and the power to do what pleases
him.

Philippians 2:13 (NLT)

Chapter 2

Define Your Desire

*She has a desire that is destined
to fail without Divine intervention*

A while ago, I decided to go deeper about living for God. What does this mean in practical terms? With my foot off the gas pedal, everything felt like an experiment because I was trying to unlearn lifelong patterns and develop new ones.

"Have A Desire That Is Destined To Fail Without Divine Intervention."

I sat with this question for months and what surprised me most during this tentative time was how much I grew to love God and genuinely love people. The Word of God was undeniably recalibrating my heart and mind, breathing life into my soul. Jesus had clearly done a work inside me. I assumed I'd been a Christian for most of my life. But I lacked the kind of transformation that only Christ can produce: a change of heart from the inside out. I began operating at a slower pace and actively sought the Lord for my next move. I learned to rely on His Holy Spirit to lead the way. I became ambitious for <u>God's will</u>, not <u>my way</u>.

I then realised that my Playing Big and Living a Rich Life had evolved. Evolved from wanting the real estate, cars, and seven figures to a collection of things I wanted to create and experience:

- I want to spend more time with my family (mum, brothers, and sisters) – so I moved closer to them and we visited almost every day.

- I want to create content, connection, and conversation that will delight and inspire people to live a beautiful life. – I was inspired to start 'The Grace Collection.'

- I want to bring healing and restoration to women like me, who would not be afraid of losing their seat at the table by identifying with Christ. Women who can talk about lovely shoes and God in the same sentence – that's why YOU'RE reading this.

- And I want to continue to cultivate my mind

But in a world that is constantly telling you what to do, who to be and what you should want, it is up to you to dig deep, explore what you intensely desire, and allow God lead you to the path of JOY.

Wired to Desire

God is a desire-creating, desire-satisfying God. Birds want to fly because God created them to do it. Dolphins want to swim because God created them with an instinct to swim. God doesn't plant wrong desires in us. When Adam first saw Eve, he discovered he had a strong desire for her. Where did that desire come from? God. God actually delights in fulfilling your desires. Though your desires may get distorted by your ego, you must learn to say no to desires that would keep you from living in the flow of God's Spirit.

> *"Are My Problems Bigger Than God,*
> *Or Is God Bigger Than My Problems?"*

Sometimes you may have to sacrifice a lesser desire for the sake of living a greater life. On the other hand, nothing makes a human being more vulnerable to temptation than a joyless life. If God removed all your desires, you wouldn't be human.

Did you know that Israeli scientists have discovered a piece of genetic code (DRD4) that may explain our primal longing for adventure? And while research is ongoing, it seems that the need for adventure is part of God's genetic design. We are adventure-seeking creatures. It's the way we're wired. We need some danger, some challenge, some risk. And the only One who can completely satisfy that human longing for adventure is the One who created us with that desire in the first place: God Himself. Any other pursuit besides your God-given desire will leave you feeling empty. Every other endeavor will leave you with a gnawing feeling that something is still missing. Why? Because everything else can be caught or accomplished, but not His Will. The Will of God is eternally indescribable. And that is why He is worthy of chasing.

> *"... Women Like Me, Who Would Not Be Afraid Of Losing Their Seat At The Table By Identifying With Christ. Women Who Can Talk About Lovely Shoes And God In The Same Sentence."*

God's plan is that every time we experience an authentic desire – a God-implanted desire – we come to understand more deeply what a good God He is. We learn how He has wired us and what He wants us to do in life, and as a result we find ourselves loving Him more and more. Do our desires sometimes lead us astray? For sure!

That's why the Bible says, *"Delight yourself also in the Lord, and He shall give you the desires of your heart.'* Psalm 37:4 NKJV

When you centre your life around God and His Word, you can trust 'the desires of your heart'. And God will give them to you!

Playing Big

The modern mystic A. W. Tozer believed that a low view of God is the cause of a hundred lesser evils, but a high view of God is the solution to ten thousand temporal problems. If that's true, and I believe it is, then your biggest problem isn't an outstanding debt, marital challenge, or a failing business. Please understand, I'm not making light of your relational, financial, or health issues. But in order to regain a godly perspective on your problems, you must answer this question: Are my problems bigger than God, or is God bigger than my problems?

Our biggest problem is our small view of God. That is the cause of all lesser evils. And a high view of God is the solution to all other problems. Until we come to the conviction that God's grace and God's power know no limits, we will not be able to ask Him for the desires of our heart – we will continue to play small. By playing small, I mean not living fully.

> *"... Once We Embrace The Omnipotence Of God, We'll Desire God-Sized Dreams."*

But once we embrace the omnipotence of God, we'll desire God-sized dreams. How big is your God?

Is He big enough to pay your bills, restore your marriage or heal your financial crises? Is He bigger than your followers, the awards or the reputation you're trying to keep? If He is bigger than all of those things, then desire for more of Him.

Claim Your Promise

Our opening scene provides an important insight that can be helpful in understanding what drives our desire.

Moses is about to make what is the most significant appointment of his career as "Master" of the Jewish people (*Moshe Rabbenu*): He is about to designate the advance reconnaissance "committee" who will investigate the "lay of the Promised Land" and bring back a report to the newly freed Hebrews wandering in the desert. This is his most crucial appointment because God had initially promised the Hebrews whilst they were still in Egypt that they were to be taken out of their bondage and brought into the Promised Land of Canaan.

I've observed that the rectification of things sometimes seems to come from humans and not from God. Look at this case. It was the women themselves who began the reform. God did not stir first. The five women gave this reform to the economy of Israel.

I'm glad to inform you as we read from the text above that desires are from God. The very idea which we think is ours is not, but God's. "He is Lord of all," of all good ideas, noble impulses, holy inspiration, sudden movements of the soul upward into higher life and broader liberty. This is His plan of training humans. He seems to stand aside, and to take no part in some obviously good movements, and we say, "This is a human movement, a political movement, a non-religious movement," not knowing what we are talking about, forgetting that the very desire out of which it all sprang came down from the Father of lights, that the very eloquence by which it is supported is Divinely taught, that the very gold which is its sinew is His: they have not gone far back enough in their investigation into the origin of things, or they would have found God in movements which are often credited to the human genres alone.

These women were asking for two things: they requested that their father be counted posthumously in the census since he had no male heir to be counted, and they asked that they be given the land that would be rightly theirs if they were sons. This land these women were asking for, they had never seen. In the earlier part of the story, the generation that went before them were fearful about entering the Promised Land and as a consequence they all died in the wilderness and did not get to enter the Promised Land.

The daughters of Zelophehad, on the other hand, believed in a land to come. They believed it was good and they wanted an inheritance there. **What Do You Want A Share Of?**

Knowledge Drives Your Desire

A friend of mine used to work in the Trust Department of a bank in Lagos, Nigeria and I've visited her on a number of occasions and witnessed some unhealthy incidents. She took her time to explain how the whole process works and voila – a perfect fit for this book.

The Trust Department is where estates and trusts are established and handled for families. If a customer dies, they may have put in their will that certain monies are put in a trust for family members. Or even before someone passes away, a person can set up a trust for one or more people. It stipulates how much money there is and how it is going to be handled and distributed.

When we refer to heirs and joint heirs, we are speaking of people who inherit the property of the person who has passed away. Sometimes, the will is read, and everyone is okay with how it will all work out, but there are times when people are not happy about their share or how it is going to be handled. I have seen people act extremely ugly over what was being inherited and to whom it was going. Some people fight over amounts of money or certain personal items. Some squabble over who is going to run the business or why an 'extra' person has been written into the will. Let's just say that money is the ultimate separator of families.

But in the Kingdom of God, we all inherit everything. We are joint heirs of the Kingdom and God set it up so that we all share in the inheritance equally.

Another way of seeing it is this: when you are looking for a job, one of the things that you look into is the benefits package that comes with the employment. Some jobs have better benefits than others. Some offer medical, dental, and optical insurance. Some even include retirement, stock options, and such. When you sign up for these benefits, these are promises that they will uphold as long as you are in their employment and stay within the guidelines given. When you sign up for these benefits, do you constantly wonder if they are telling the truth? You may look at your pay slip every once in a while, as a cautionary measure, which is practical to do, to see that it is coming out of your cheque. And you should check your account to make sure the money is being deposited. Essentially, you believe that these benefits or promises are being kept by your employer.

God has benefits as well when you "sign up" to go on this adventure spree with Him. Check His 'handbook', you might just find what you're looking for.

Although few details are given about the sisters themselves, further research provides a portrait of intelligent and pious women. The sisters' intelligence is evident from their clear presentation of their case. Indeed, God Himself endorsed their argument, saying, "Zelophehad's daughters are right. Give them land …" (Numbers 27:6 MSG)

Desire can be seasonal

In the Book of Esther, we see God's plan to put a young woman in a place of influence years before she or anyone else knew that that influence would save not only her life, but the lives of a nation of people.

Esther had been taken from her home where she was raised, to the home of her cousin Mordecai, who took her in when her parents died. She was Jewish but Mordecai had advised her to hide her ethnicity and religion. She was cut off from her family and her culture. She was at the mercy of the king who did not understand her or who she was. When a plan of total annihilation of the Jewish race was created by a favored adviser of the king, Esther did not just pray and watch God move, she appeared before the King with boldness and presented her desire – "…if I perish, I perish."(Esther 4:16 KJV)

You are in your place of influence because God has put you there. You are the influencer in YOUR world, whether that is in the office, in the school, as an at-home mom, with your family, in the gym or wherever it is you are. You have been moved into that position for such a time as this. Just as Esther had to be bold to work at being what was expected of her as a royal, you must put the work into **being** who God wants you to be for His Kingdom. Let people know who you are and whose you are - for such a time as this.

Fuel for Desire

The reason you have such a strong desire to accomplish something in life is because God created you to 'do it'. Your capacity to desire certain things is a gift from God; it's a powerful motivator. Picture two ladies taking swimming lessons. One does it because she watched the Olympic Games and wants to win a gold medal in the future. The other is also going to the Olympics but she takes lessons because her husband said she had to. Which lady do you think will put her all into the lessons?

In Genesis we read: 'Jacob served seven [*more*] years to get Rachel, but they seemed like only a few days to him because of his love for her' (Genesis 29:20 NIV). What kind of person would see seven years' hard work as a mere few days? Someone working towards his or her dream!

A strong career drive accompanied by the desire to learn and achieve can be good things, unless they lead to workaholism, worshipping status, neglecting prayer, and manipulating other people. Though the Bible is clear that we are to "work with all our heart," it's equally clear that our "motives are weighed by the Lord" (Proverbs 16:2 NIV). When that happens, you need to re-evaluate your motivation. But if that's not the case and you find yourself growing in God with a fire inside you to accomplish something – go forth and

41

achieve. He is with you. After all, He sent you. He put the fire in you.

"What Kind Of Person Would See Seven Years' Hard Work As A Mere Few Days? Someone Working Towards His Or Her Dream!"

In my case, I understood later after working with a therapist that at the root of my perpetual drive for success was the perpetual fear of failure, which I found was traceable to my upbringing.

What is your heart's motivation for life?

Maybe you haven't ever thought about this before. That's okay; but now is the time to do so. What deep, inner desire drives you or will drive you through life?

You don't have to let your flesh decide this. You can decide it with your spirit, by the influence of the precious Holy Spirit.

I challenge you to do this.

I urge you to do this.

I DARE you to do this.

What is your heart's motivation going to be? Decide; then write it down.

After you do, you can use the motivation you choose as a compass for everything you do for the rest of your life. It will make all the difference in the world.

Will you do it?

Okay, so you're ready and eager to have some huge desires but you don't know where to begin. The truth is, you can't teach people how to conceive great ideas because they're supposed to be given by God. But I think there are several strategies that you can train yourself in to be able to birth them. Here are some nuggets to get you started.

1. Fantasise about what turns you on – I enjoy meditation and my calmness and I'll just allow my soul to fly.

2. Keep a journal. Don't just keep them, go back and read what you've written

3. Detach yourself from a problem and use the 'balcony view' approach. Not sure who created this approach, but it simply means you step back from the dance floor, go to the balcony and watch people dance. I've found this approach very useful even to manage my emotions.

4. Remove this word *'can't'* from your vocabulary. This doesn't mean saying YES to everything, but it forces you to imagine the wackiest solution possible – even if you're perceived as crazy.

5. Be bold enough to disrupt your routine. It has been said that we live on an auto pilot life most of

the time, that's why we're not able to tap into our deeper level and get those innovative ideas. When was the last time you changed your route to work? When was the last time you walked through the park and not sit on a bench?

DELILAH

You'll find her mentioned in poems and stage plays, television shows and movie scripts. Even a writer wrote a song that ends with the warning, "There's a little of Delilah in each and every gal."

Delilah a woman whose desire was bone deep.

Was she beautiful? Perhaps, though she's not described in bible.

Was she cunning? Of course! Though she didn't bother to hide her plans to trap Samson.

The thing is: the rulers of the Philistines urged Delilah to "lure" Samson into revealing the source of his strength. These men didn't mince words. "Entice him" they said. Other versions of the bible said: "Seduce him" "trick him" "deceive him."

How much did the men offer her for this deception? Can you guess? Eleven hundred shekels of silver each. Since the Philistines were led by five men of equal authority, that adds up to a boatload of cash. In modern money, about fifteen million dollars!

Well for Delilah, it was no contest. The money trumped the man.

Did she finally get what she wanted? Yes, she did - Judges 16:18.

Let me ask you, what would you be willing to do to manifest your desire?

YOUR GUIDE TO THE FUTURE

Trait 2 – DESIRE

1. Search deep in your heart – what is it you believe God has given you to do on this earth? Remember, He creates DESIRES in us. It has to be what ONLY GOD can help you to achieve and it is usually far out, too big and somewhat 'amazing' for you to accomplish. Therefore God is the ONLY One who can help you achieve it.

2. Be very CLEAR about your DESIRE. Don't dumb it down. DESCRIBE and DEFINE it with as much ACCURACY as you can. Write it down.

3. PRAY about it.

4. Study about it. Go get all the knowledge you can about it.

5. Notice if your DESIRE can be fulfilled by you – that is, without God's help. If so, erase it.

6. Go back to the sub-heading *'What Is Your Heart's Motivation For Life?'* in the book and follow the 5 nuggets I share to help you get and make this DESIRE a reality.

Trait 3

She has Audacious FAITH

Now faith is the assurance of things hoped
for, the conviction of things not seen.
Hebrews 11:1 (ESV)

"Faith is the external elixir which gives life, power and action to the impulse of thought! Faith is the starting point of all accumulation of riches! Faith is the basis of all miracles and all mysteries which cannot be analysed by the rules of science! Faith is the only known antidote for failure!"

-Napoleon Hill

"Faith is taking the first step even when you don't see the whole staircase."

-Martin Luther King, Jr.

Chapter 3

It is indescribable

After building a successful career in the telecommuni-cations industry, Lyn resigned her job and decided to move to a remote town. When her former client heard of this, they reached out to her with an irresistible offer, but she declined. The client promised to leave the offer open for three months in case she changed her mind.

I remember speaking to her on the phone, curious and concerned about her decision. It's not uncommon for people to leave their jobs and travel out of the country, but not to a remote town. So, getting through to her on the phone was a big deal to me – I wanted to know what went wrong.

"So Where Are We Going?' You May Ask.
That Is What All Followers Want To Know.
This Is What Leaders Pretend To Be Sure Of."

"Seriously Aji, I'm not sure what I'm going to do now, but I have a strong leading that I should resign and come to this town," she told me. I honestly didn't believe Lyn and I wasn't prepared to add this to my already full plate. Lyn later got a job with the local government business bureau, five years later she went on an exchange programme out of the country where she met her husband. They've been happily married for nine years and have three children.

"Faith Is Intangible; It Can't Be Articulated And Can't Be Explained. It Is Something That Just Is."

No matter where the ultimate destination might be, the ability to determine the course is the most essential element needed for achieving our dreams. 'So where are we going?' You may ask. That is what all followers want to know. This is what leaders pretend to be sure of. The reality is that most people who walk by faith have difficulty answering that one dreadful question. They have difficulty because faith is an abstract and the question is asking for a concrete answer. Faith is intangible; it can't be articulated and can't be explained. It is something that just is.

Faith is that thing, that place, that indescribable something that we pursue without fully being able to explain to others the unique drive we have towards it. It is that inner feeling, that says, "Yes, I am looking out for something. There is something in here for me. I do not know exactly what it is but when I see it, I will know it." How will you know? Quite honestly, I am not sure. All I know is that when it is in front of me, I will know that this is it. What I am saying is that there is a compass in our souls that inform us inwardly when it is the right man, the right woman, or whatever it is we pursue.

Faith is a necessary part of fulfilling your God-idea or anything else for that matter. It is that which gives God a go-ahead to do as you wish it to do. You see, you cannot be bold without faith, for such becoming is temporary. You cannot be happy if you are unsure that you are happy. You also cannot create goals without faith, not only in their accuracy but also in their coming to reality for you. Even speaking and acting without faith is powerless.

Lyn's story is a pretty cool picture and a good reminder that you don't have to see the whole staircase ... sometimes you just step out in faith and go for it! Each step you take reveals the next step. But we all know the first step is the hardest. It often requires that you break out of your comfort zone and overcome the inertia of standing still. The good news is inertia works both ways. Yes, it is hard to get going but once you create that initial momentum, the effort to keep going gets easier and easier. And creating that initial momentum, breaking out of your comfort zone and overcoming the inertia of standing still all require faith. Without faith there is no FIRST step.

"Even Speaking And Acting Without Faith Is Powerless."

Many teachers have written books on faith. This isn't new. But now you will see why they have always taught this, and you will see how to create and expand your faith, something that has so far been elusive to many people.

But remember, as you read on, that faith is a lot like state, **being**. You cannot only speak faith, you also need to **do** faith, and be faith-full. And the way to do that is to simply decide to be faith, just like that, and let no other contradiction come to you. I hope this gets clearer and easier as we proceed.

Faith is unseen

Let us examine the faith that these five young women, the daughters of Zelophehad, possessed with regard to the promised inheritance. You must remember that the children of Israel were still in the wilderness. They had not seen the Promised Land, but God had made a covenant with them that they should possess it. He had declared that He would bring them into a land which flowed with milk and honey and there, plant them and that that land should belong to them and to their descendants forever. Now these women had faith in this heritage. Exodus 6:6-8 (KJV)

They were not like Esau, who thought so little of the inheritance which was his birthright that he sold it to his brother Jacob for a mess of pottage, Genesis 25:29-34 (KJV), but they believed it to be worth having. They regarded it, though they had never beheld it, as being something exceedingly substantial, and so looking upon it, they were afraid lest they should be left out when the land was divided. Though they had not seen it yet, being persuaded that it was somewhere and the children of Israel would have it in due time, their anxiety was this: lest they, having no brothers, should be forgotten in the distribution and so lose the right to their inheritance. They had a holy expectation of an unseen inheritance and they were anxious to get their portion of it.

These women asked by faith, and God graciously and lovingly honored their desire.

Faith is active

These women were single women. They could have played the victim card and moped about being orphans with no brothers and no land. They could have gone from tent to tent complaining. They could have rushed into marriage to solve their problem themselves. But they did not. These were noble, godly women who trusted that God would provide for them and were willing to boldly step outside their comfort zone to see this happen. They trusted the leadership of Moses and believed God would be gracious and just towards them and because of their faith – they were protected against fear.

Do we have this sort of faith? Sometimes I am tempted to talk about my fears or complain about them rather than face them with faith – head on. We must not run from things that are hard – especially when we know we are doing what is right. Let's be inspired by these women today and ask God to be used for change in this world!

Faith brings about change

These five women had the courage to approach leaders to make a change! As a result of their faith, they were given a portion just the same as the men. They not only gained an inheritance for themselves but for ALL women, in this situation, for generations to come!

Do we have this sort of faith? These women understood that without faith we cannot please God. (Hebrews 11:6 KJV) They were young and focused. Life had dealt them a difficult hand as they had suffered a huge loss without their father's protection.

But clearly, this father had raised them to walk with the Lord and to have faith. They knew right from wrong which is why their request was granted by the Lord. Their case set a precedent and expanded the legal rights of women. Due to the ruling regarding them, women were included in the list of eligible heirs of property. The following became the inheritance order: son, daughter, brother, paternal uncle, and nearest clan kin. Property was not to be transferred outside of one's tribe. Numbers 27: 8-11(KJV)

Persistence breeds faith

I love the parable of the persistent widow. I don't mean any disrespect, but I think 'persistent' is a nice word for 'crazy.' This woman was crazy, but when the cause is a righteous one, it's a holy crazy! We aren't told what injustice took place, but she was on a mission. Maybe her son was falsely imprisoned for a crime he didn't commit. Maybe the man who molested her daughter was still on the streets. We don't know for sure. But whatever it was, she wouldn't take 'NO' for an answer. And the judge knew it. The judge knew there was no quitting for this crazy woman. Does the Judge know that about you?

You can use persistence to increase your faith. By persisting, even when it looks like you should give up, you can increase your faith and bring about the outcome you desire. This is a conscious decision you make because faith enables persistence. It is a tight circle. You cannot achieve much if you are not persistent, if you keep telling yourself things are not going to work out. Persistence is a slight step ahead of faith in that you can use it to build faith, but every step that persistence takes has to be followed by a step in faith. Persistence, literally, pays. Nothing is truly impossible.

Faith Trusts

Not knowing what one wishes to have clearly is a major cause of doubt and disbelief. First, Mahlah and her sisters believed God's promise that they would enter the land and enjoy physical blessings there. We, in the Church Age have been promised that we have been blessed with "every spiritual blessing in the heavenly places in Christ" - Ephesians 1:3b (NKJV). God's Word tells us these blessings are ours now. Do you believe that the life Jesus gives is everlasting, not probational or conditional? Do you believe God's promise that you have been sealed by the Holy Spirit and that you are positionally in Christ? Are you enjoying the spiritual blessings that God has said are already yours?

I've come to realise that sometimes blessings do not come until we have walked a painful road, until we have consistently prayed to God as a co-creator to bring about a change, until we step out in faith – way outside our comfort zone – and watch God work through us, despite our weaknesses. Blessings do not come until we have the courage to confront something that is wrong, in order to make it right.

Will you dare to challenge something in this world that you know is wrong and push to make it right? Are you willing to make a difference for generations to come? Are you willing to step out in faith today?

"Everything about faith involves the unseen. As humans, we operate primarily in the realm of the seen, the physical. We draw conclusions from what we see or do not see.

A man is considered wealthy when he drives an expensive car. A woman is considered beautiful based on her physical appearance and the decision to court her is sometimes based solely on that.

We take advice from people who have thousands of followers on Instagram- they must have something we need we conclude.

While there is some element of truth in these examples, it isn't always true. What you see isn't always indicative of what it appears to be.

Faith does not rely on what we see. Faith is a spiritual exercise that is anchored only by hope. Another unseen element. If you are going to live by faith, then you must ignore the physical and start to live by your spirit which is one with God"

Credit: A write up by Toks Aruoture from the Living from the Inside Out' collection of writings

YOUR GUIDE TO THE FUTURE

Trait 3 – AUDACIOUS FAITH

Following on from Traits 1 and 2, DEVELOP your FAITH

Do the following steps one after the another.

Do not go to the next step until you have done the one before.

1. THINK about the INVISIBLE.
2. THINK about the fact that you CANNOT see FAITH. Sit quietly and THINK about this.
3. Then, THINK about the fact that you bring things into REALITY through your FAITH.
4. Now, do FAITH. BELIEVE God for your DESIRE.
5. PRACTICE FAITH daily by reading chunks of chapters of the Bible DAILY because FAITH COMES BY HEARING AND HEARING BY THE WORD.

Trait 4

She is Prayerful

"Pray without ceasing."

1 Thessalonians 5:17 (KJV)

Chapter 4

What does it mean to pray ceaselessly?

She adds to her desires, faithful and constant prayers.

T hink about this: it has been said that even before you ask, it is given unto you. It has also been said that ask and it shall be given unto you. Do you catch that? Asking is not begging, you do not beg God, for it is already given to you even before you ask. Begging simply means you lack something and you're desperate for it. Begging puts you in a state of neediness, someone told me that a while back. Begging is not even God's idea.

> *"... Prayer Is Not Something You Do Once*
> *At A Special Time During The Day And Act*
> *Totally Different And Confused The Rest*
> *Of The Day. It Is A Lifestyle."*

Here then is what it means to pray ceaselessly:

You come **boldly** to the throne of grace wholeheartedly with your *desire*; you **pray** it to come into being, and you have *faith* in God to make it manifest. And because you know this works, because of your faith and consistency, it will take form in the most unexpected and miraculous of ways. That is prayer.

Praying without ceasing is going through the whole day, every day, with such focused intention and attention for all your life's desires, with a depth of assurance and a grateful heart.

No rules here

Contrary to what we were taught while growing up, prayer is not something you do once at a special time during the day and act totally different and confused the rest of the day. It is a lifestyle. Prayer is meant to be active, ever present, and part of your normal everyday life. It is co-creating with God; it wills to action, it is self-assertive. It is not the periodic, passive, helpless, and emotional appeal that many of us were taught as children. I'll urge you to get rid of the idea that prayer is the same as begging God for a favor, and God chooses whether to grant this favor and comes down and does both your work and His. Prayer is actually will, will that is co-creative and your part in it is to have a clear desire and faith.

Sometimes prayer is a casual conversation with God. It's like two friends catching up over coffee. But sometimes, prayer involves intense intercession, as it was when Jesus prayed in Gethsemane on the eve of His crucifixion. It was so intense that Jesus was literally sweating drops of blood. He was facing the greatest test of His life on earth, so He prayed through the night. Three times He prayed a prayer of consecration: "My Father, if it is possible, may this cup be taken from Me. Yet not as I will, but as you will." Matthew 26:39 (NKJV)

"... If We Aren't Willing To Risk Our Reputation, We'll Never Establish God's Reputation. "

There is no criterion by which God decides to grant or not to grant prayers. Prayer is an inward energetic process, a call you give out with a holy expectation of an answer, without a shred of doubt. It is a strong and certain will. When you realise that the Granter is the one that gives you the desire of your heart, you will truly be praying and receiving without fail. For your prayers will be of pure gratitude for what already is given unto you even before you ask. Just be grateful and smile!

How Hungry Are You?

During one of my Mum's visits to London, she quickly observed that my son was a fussy eater. 'Mother's guilt' made me pamper Alex excessively with different types of food but he'd almost all the time waste it. When I get back and ask if Alex had eaten, my Mum would say; *"leave him to be really hungry."*

I didn't buy into this at first but later decided to give it a go. It was shocking to see that Alex would finish his meal and even sleep off at the table – I think he was probably too tired from being hungry.

> ### *"It's The Impossible Prayer Requests That Honor God Because They Reveal Our Faith And Allow God To Reveal His Glory."*

I feel the reason why most people don't pray is because they are not hungry enough. There is an adage: 'Desperate times call for desperate measures.'

Every prayer is a calculated risk, but sometimes God calls us to ante up all the faith we have, and then let the chips fall where they may!

When we act in faith, we aren't risking our reputation; we are risking God's reputation because He's the one who made the promise in the first place. But if we aren't willing to risk our reputation, we'll never establish God's reputation.

One day, a lady was sharing her audacious ideas with me when I asked her; "Have you prayed about it?" She looked at me in amazement and wondered why she'll even bring that to God. She thought it was a crazy idea that she was just sharing with me. I asked her what gave her the assurance that God wasn't listening – then we both smiled.

Why do we mistakenly think that God is offended by our prayers for the impossible? I think that God is offended by anything less! God is offended when we ask Him to do things, we can do ourselves. It's the impossible prayer requests that honor God because they reveal our faith and allow God to reveal His glory.

In Luke 11, Jesus tells a story about a man who won't take 'NO' for an answer. He keeps knocking on his friend's door until he gets what he came for. It's a parable about prevailing in prayer. And Jesus honors his bold determination: "...yet because of your shameless audacity he will surely get up and give you as much as you need." – Luke 11:8 (NIV) I love this depiction of prayer. That expression, 'shameless audacity' says it all. There are times when you need to do whatever it takes. You need to grab hold of the horns of the altar and not let go. You need to do something crazy, something risky, something different. You need to demonstrate your hunger!

Don't murmur, pass it on

A child was crying passionately, and I heard the mother say, "If you cry for nothing, I will soon give you something to cry for." From the sound of her palm on his bottom, I gathered the moral is that those who cry about nothing are making a rod for their own backs and will probably be made to smart for it.

Going back to our scene in chapter 1, I must commend them yet again for the way in which these women went about their business. I do not find that they went complaining from tent to tent that they were afraid that they had no portion. Many people do that; they tell their doubts and fears to others, but they get no further. But these five women went straight to Moses. He was their head; he was their mediator and then it is said that "Moses brought their cause before the LORD." – Numbers 27:5 (KJV). You see, these women did not try to get what they wanted by force. They did not say, "We will take care to get our share of the land when we get there", but they went straight to Moses and Moses took their cause and laid it before the Lord.

Do you have a crazy idea? Go straight to Jesus our Mediator and Jesus will take your cause and lay it before the Lord! Did you catch that?

Take it out of your own hands and put into the hands of the prophet like unto Moses, and you will surely succeed!

Now, observe *the success of these women.* The Lord accepted their plea, for He said unto Moses, "The daughters of Zelophehad speak right." (Numbers 27:7 KJV) And then God said that these sisters should have their portion just the same as the men had; that they should have their share of land just as if they had inherited it as sons.

Yes, and when you pray to Him and when His dear Son takes your prayer to Him, God will say, "That lady speaks rightly."

The patience of the planter

Each prayer is like a seed that gets planted in the ground. It disappears for a season, but it eventually bears fruit that blesses future generations. In fact, our prayers bear fruit forever. Even when we die, our prayers don't. Each prayer takes on a life, an eternal life, of its own. Because we are surrounded by technologies that make our lives faster and easier, we tend to think about spiritual realities in technological terms. We want to reap the very second we sow. We want God to microwave answers, and tweet instructions. We want things to happen at the speed of light instead of the speed of a seed planted in the ground, yet almost all spiritual realities in Scripture are described in agricultural terms.

We want our dreams to become reality overnight. We want our prayers answered immediately. But that isn't the way it works in God's kingdom. **We need the patience of the planter. We need the foresight of the farmer. We need the mind-set of the sower.**

"We Need The Patience Of The Planter. We Need The Foresight Of The Farmer. We Need The Mind-Set Of The Sower."

We worry about outcomes instead of focusing on input. We cannot make things grow. Period. All we can do is plant and water. But if we plant and water, God promises to give the increase. This is both bad news and good news. We cannot break the law of sowing and reaping any more than we can break the law of gravity. No farmer would plant beans and expect to harvest corn! If you sow kindness, you will reap kindness. If you sow generosity, you will reap generosity. If you sow love, you will reap love.

All of us go through times of spiritual, relational, or financial famine. It seems like the harvest will never come. And the temptation is to stop planting, but my advice is simple: sow a seed. Keep praying, keep obeying, keep giving, keep loving, keep serving. And if you keep sowing the right seeds, the harvest of blessing will come in God's time, in God's way!

How desperate are you for the blessing, the breakthrough, the miracle? Desperate enough to pray through the night? How many times are you willing to claim the promise? Until the day you die? How long will you knock on the door of opportunity? Until your knuckles are raw? Until you knock the door down?

YOUR GUIDE TO THE FUTURE

Trait 4 – PRAYERFUL

Set alarms on your phone, alarms to go off to PRAY and to PRAISE.

Create 3 alarms to PRAY regarding your DESIRE.

Create 3 alarms to PRAISE God regarding your DESIRE.

Do it this way:

Alarm 1 – PRAY
Alarm 2 - PRAISE
Alarm 3 – PRAY
Alarm 4 - PRAISE
Alarm 5 – PRAY
Alarm 6 – PRAISE

*Spend only 5 minutes each time.

Set the alarms from morning until evening, so that you can take 5-minute breaks to ACTION the alarms even if you are at work.

BE DILIGENT to respond to these alarms.

It will not do you any good if you all you do is set the alarms and not ACT on them.

This then is 'praying without ceasing'.

Trait 5

She lives a RICH LIFE

"My purpose is to give them
a rich and satisfying life."

John 10:10 (NLT)

Chapter 5

A rich and satisfying life

I was burdened one morning with this scripture which later became one of my favorites, *"My purpose is to give you a rich and satisfying life – John 10:10"*. If you know me or have been following my posts, you'll know that my entire life revolves around this scripture, but I didn't get here in one day.

Prior to that morning, I had been burdened with so many challenges that just appeared too complicated and it just seemed as the days became weeks, months and years, more and more mini devils crept in. So here I am waiting on the Lord and He lit this up in my spirit; *"Aji I have given you a rich and satisfying life, will you receive it?"* I kept quiet while nodding *'yes'* with the knowledge that my life seemed a lot less than satisfying. Did I miss something in what He said? So, I read again; *"The thief's purpose is to steal and kill and destroy. My purpose is to give them a rich and satisfying life."*

I quickly looked up the meaning of 'rich' and 'abundance' in the dictionary; (note that another translation refers to 'abundance') it means *'present in great quantity; more than adequate; over sufficient, well and richly supplied.'*

The richest man that had ever lived - King Solomon put it nicely when he wrote *"I said to myself, 'Come on, let's try pleasure. Let's look for the 'good things' in life.' But I found that this, too, was meaningless."* - Ecclesiastes 2:1 (NLT) That doesn't sound rich and satisfying, now does it? Now I became more confused and decided to read the whole of John chapter 10 for more understanding and to grasp what Jesus really said about this rich life?

In the earlier verses of John 10, Jesus is speaking in Jerusalem, a city where shepherds would bring their flocks into the walls at night. Inside the city would be a common pen where the sheep would be kept. This common pen is called a "sheepfold". It would be surrounded by a large wall with a single gated entrance. A gatekeeper would be on guard to be sure no thief scaled over the wall and only the shepherds were allowed inside.

Several flocks would be housed together and when the shepherd came for his flock, he would call them by a certain name or whistle in a certain manner. Only those sheep that belonged to him would respond. The others would remain in the pen. Rather remarkable, right?

Jesus compares himself to the gate protecting the sheepfold. He also states that *"all who came before me were thieves and robbers"* – John 10:8 (NLT). So, who were these thieves and robbers? There is no indication that He is referring to Satan. He is referring to those who would use deception to lead the sheep that belonged to Jesus astray. He is referring to the false prophets and the teachers of the law. But He makes the claim that those selected to be his sheep did not listen to this deception.

Let's read His verdict here: "*Yes, I am the gate. Those who come in through me will be saved. They will come and go freely and will find good pastures. The thief's purpose is to steal and kill and destroy. My purpose is to give them a rich and satisfying life.*" (John 10:9-10 NLT)

> ### "People Are Not Poor Because God Is Poor. People Are Poor Because Their Abundance Consciousness Is Poor."

Here is the thing: a rich and satisfying life is a life where we are safe, free, and blessed. A rich and satisfying life is one free of worry (*just imagine the relationship between the sheep and the shepherd*).

Reflecting on this scripture that has been in existence for over 2000 years; I then began to understand why living a rich life or in abundance is now thrown around by life coaches and woo-woo authors? – And people pay a heck of a lot of money to have that promised life. They have equated 'a rich and satisfying life' with material things alone and money in the bank. I've been there so I understand, and it's taken me years to really grasp what it really means.

Being Rich

Just as boldness is a state, so is 'being rich'. Being rich is who you are – I struggled to grasp this – Yes, I confess. When you're in massive debt, it's difficult to feel rich let alone 'be rich.' But if we learn from the farmer, every revelation from God is a seed, water it and it'll surely bring harvest. If you believe that you are made in the image and after the likeness of God, then abundance and affluence are your natural states. Your spirit already knows this to be true. **All you need is to remember this as often as you can to experience what you truly are.**

I've come to understand this truth: God has more than enough business and wealth for everyone. Way more than enough. People are not poor because God is poor. People are poor because their abundance consciousness is poor. Even in a billion lifetimes, let alone one lifetime, you cannot possibly use up all the wealth given to you freely by God. But you can "fail" to receive it by your own thoughts, words, actions, and, most of all, your chosen state of being and truths that you uphold about yourself.

Enough to go around

A friend of mine used to be over-protective of me and my ideas, she **felt** I shared too much with people and on social media. Sometimes she'll come to me and say things like, 'Aji this person copied you, and this person you shared with is now doing what you said.' Some of those were quite what happened, and it bothered me a bit, so I took it to God in prayer.

This is it: No one is going to "take your share" or "beat you to it." There is more than enough for everyone. **The only time there is not enough, the only time when you are "beaten to it" is when you think and act competitively instead of thinking and acting creatively and trusting in the abundant nature of God.**

Economics teaches about scarcity of resources. I seriously don't believe that is true! That is why it is failing to apply to New Economy businesses and calculations today. Economics was "invented" at a time when people believed in scarcity now, we hardly hear people talk about that anymore. We are only now beginning to see that certain resources can never run out. For example, software, music, or other digital content downloaded or broadcast cannot run out. How do you run out of a software download? No matter how many copies you download, there still remains that original copy that everyone is downloading. One copy multiplies as much as is needed without costing the maker any more money.

Pay your dues

After paying off my debt, I got used to seeing money in my bank account. I remember one morning, I called my friend and was so excited to see money in my account, I hadn't experienced that in a long, long time. I liked it. I liked it so much that I struggled to pay my bills. Not that I didn't have the money to pay, I just didn't want the money to leave my bank account.

Thanks to the Holy Spirit Who quickly rebuked me that, that was a scarcity and lack mindset. I later realised that it was negative energy that I had to intentionally deal with. The Holy Spirit taught me that paying my bills on time is a message I send to God that I am responsible and ready to be trusted with more.

Can God trust you with more?

Thoughts of scarcity take abundance away from your life. They manifest scarcity. You can get temporarily rich this way, but you cannot rise to your full potential this way, and indeed, you may even fail. So, I encourage you to spend your money gladly, cheerfully, and with excitement. Whether you are buying items or paying bills, be glad that you are doing it. Money runs away from those who feel it is scarce, those who have negativity toward its use.

Life invests in you when you invest in self

I remembered one of my visits to the city of Dubai in the United Arab Emirates – known for luxury shopping, ultramodern architecture and a lively nightlife scene. It was a beautiful experience with family and my friend Dee, but something happened!

> *"Money Runs Away From Those Who Feel It Is Scarce, Those Who Have Negativity Toward Its Use."*

I had walked by different Diamond stores including the Graff store (*the store with the most fabulous jewels in the world*) on New Bond Street in London for years, but would never let myself go in. I admired the stones from afar.

I would watch women through the shop's glass doors checking out pieces of jewelry like they would fruits at the grocery store – "waste of time and money" I'll say, to comfort myself.

So, during my visit to the Emirates, I summoned the courage to indulge my fantasies. I decided to treat myself to a diamond. Diamond!

When the Jeweler handed me the machine and I pressed the payment button on a pair of very expensive diamond earrings, I felt like throwing up, and my tummy started rumbling.

My heart was saying, "Jump, Aji!"

But my brain was streaming out all kinds of fear tactics:

"It's a waste of money."

"You're making someone else rich."

"You don't belong there."

"Who in the world do you think you are?"

With shaking hands, I grabbed the diamond from the jeweler and quickly left the store before I changed my mind.

That day...

- I knew deep down that everything I desired was not going to be found in fear and lack.
- Deep down I knew that everything I wanted was not going to be found by doing the same things over and over.

Let's face it: a diamond doesn't change a woman.

However, here's what I've discovered:

When a woman is willing to invest in herself, life begins to invest in her. For me, it will be a reminder of that woman who finally gathered the courage to buy a diamond.

Contrary to popular belief, investing in self is not a waste, it's not about the thing and it is not about the price either…it is about the act, the courage and the belief to do so. It's about honoring the 'god' 'the divine' in self. Let me shed a bit more light in the next few pages.

Love is the catalyst

One thing I really struggled with after my divorce was experiencing love. When people would talk about love I would keep quiet because I was tired of defending whether it exists or not. I shared what I was going through with an ex-colleague who also pastored a church and he sent me a book through the post, *Love: The Way to Victory* by Kenneth E. Hagin. I read this book in one night and prayed using what I had learnt from it. For the first time in months, I slept like a baby and woke up refreshed. I couldn't recollect how many times I read that book in a week but what I do know is that something drastically changed in me.

Many people think of love as an emotion that comes and goes. In one moment, we feel intense love and in the next we feel nothing at all. We may then become consumed by doubts about our relationships or get caught up in an anxious search for love, striving to attract someone who will finally give us the love and approval we've longed for. But in truth, love isn't a capricious emotion but a state of being. I came to grasp the understanding that my true nature is **LOVE.**

It is an experience of unity with all creation. In every moment we can choose to be the presence of love and let that love guide all our words and actions. This choice will transform all your relationships, including the one with yourself.

While still learning how to cultivate these loving relationships, I noticed these wonderful experiences would come and go and sometimes took time to come back again, so I went to the Lord for help.

In His Presence

There is a saying that goes: 'When the **student is ready, the teacher will appear**.' Not sure of who came up with it, though I think it's a key concept to keep in mind. I believe the prayer I prayed in that quiet room is a demonstration that I was ready, thus anytime I approach the throne of grace, help is there waiting. So, in my quest to understand my 'short circuited' love experiences; the Lord whispered this scripture in my ears: *You make known to me the path of life; in your presence there is fullness of joy; at your right hand are pleasures forevermore.* Ps 16:11. (ESV).

""God, Whatever It Is That I'm Doing, I'm Going To Do It For You." That's When Your Life Becomes An Act Of Worship."

What does it mean to be in His presence? You see, so many of us Christians compartmentalise life by saying, "here's my worship hour" or "I do that when I go to church once a week." Here's my Bible study hour...I go to a small group once a week." And then over here in the next compartment, I've got my job. And over here in this compartment, I've got my social life. And down here in this compartment, I've got my family life. I was guilty too.

While I was battling with this whole idea of His presence, Colossians 1:16 quickly came to my rescue - *...for through him God created everything in heaven and on earth, the seen and the unseen things, including spiritual powers, lords, rulers, and authorities. God created the whole universe through him and for him.* (GNT)

Wow!

It was as though scales fell off my eyes and words cannot describe the truth of this reality.

Simply put, being in His Presence means seeing 'the divine' 'God' in everyone and everything. Though each of us appears to be a separate individual, we are all inextricably connected. This is the divinity in all life. We are all expressions and extensions of God. When we relate with each other from the level of self, it is easy to get caught up in the struggle for control and approval and the need to be right. But when we relate to each other from 'His presence', we experience increased love, joy, compassion, and harmony. This is what the Indian greeting Namasté means: the divine consciousness in me acknowledges the divine consciousness in you.

In other words, what is the picture that comes to mind when you think of being in His presence? It is focusing your mind, your thoughts, and your attention on God. It is seeing God everyday, your sleeping, eating, commuting to work, and this helps turn the mundane, trivial things that don't seem to mean a whole lot into pure joy. It means, "God, whatever it is that I'm doing, I'm going to do it for You." That's when your life becomes an act of worship.

From this perspective, you'll be able to use your ability to accomplish good things for others. Whether you're contributing to a meeting, adding value to a team, or formulating ideas, you'll know it's more than just you. You then develop relational skills that enable you to bond with others irrespective of your personalities, you can pray for them and bless them. As you experience joy in your achievements, your life is pleasing to God.

YOUR GUIDE TO THE FUTURE

Trait 5 – LIVE A RICH and SATISFYING LIFE

1. Study what LOVE – the LOVE of God is. Get a book, eg I Dared To Call Him Father by Bilquis Sheikh and read it. Get other books on the Love of God and read them.

2. Read 1Corinthians 13:1-end and other scriptures on the Love of God DAILY.

3. Cultivate your Love for God. Consciously, intentionally and actively.

4. Accept what 2Corinthians 8:9 says by studying it and meditating on it.

5. Accept what 2Corinthians 9:8 says by studying it and meditating on it.

Take your time.

The RICH and SATISFYING LIFE is found in LOVE.

Love of God and Love for God and people.

For God is LOVE.

Chapter 6

The Concept of 'His Lady'

Nothing can quite prepare you for the overwhelming *(and beautiful)* emotions you experience when the love of your life interrupts your life. If you fancy watching love flicks *(think The Notebook, Titanic and Twilight)* as much as I do, and you love as much as I love, you'll know there really is nothing better in this world than **LOVE**.

But seriously...

One desire I pray for you to have is the desire and a burning passion to do His will. The same heartfelt prayer I prayed in that quiet room that keeps echoing in my ears even today. *"God I want to do your will, I am ambitious for you"* and I bet He knows when you're honest about it. The only thing is that, that prayer comes with a price.

> *"... Our Miracle Is Never In What We Lost – It's In What We Have Left!"*

Let's face it; we all go through times where we feel we're losing everything. A failed marriage, loss of a job, illness, unbearable debt, betrayal, the list is endless. On the outside, it might seem you've lost everything that's valuable. But the truth is, *are they really valuable?*

When I think of how I took a loan from the bank, emptied my credit cards, and withdrew all my savings to buy a house in a prime area in Africa, I shipped furnishings as well as an SUV to use in our new home. Only for my ex to walk away with them with a message saying, "Go and bring proof that you own them." Even when I went to the realtor, they told me the property was in his name so they couldn't help.

All the above and even more became my experience and I wondered what else God wanted from me? It's taken me a long time to learn and an even longer time to realize the truth that our miracle is never in what we lost – **it's in what we have left!**

Let me ask you?

- What if God hasn't placed value where you have?
- Could it be that your next level is hidden in what you have left?

Remember the widow with a handful of meal? The widow with one last jar of oil, the boy with two fish and five loaves of bread? My friend, whatever you have right now; **THAT'S ALL YOU NEED!**

I believe that where God is taking you, you don't need the weight and the extra baggage of blessings you've been holding on to or grieving over. He is **PRUNING** your life so that you carry only what you need to get out where He wants you to go, because He knows that your past blessing can become a trap and graveyard for your future. You have the capacity to improve upon and increase what you have left – there's life in it.

"... You Can Make A Living While Making A Life..."

Like a bride walking towards the altar to meet her betrothed, I say, 'YES' to be **HIS LADY**!

I say, 'YES' every day to the adventure of being used by God.

I say, 'YES' to being okay not knowing the answer but trusting His leading.

I say, 'YES' to be **HIS LADY**!

Since saying 'YES' – embracing daily and not fighting it, it's been an amazing and joyful experience. My life has taken on a whole new purpose so much more fulfilling than anything I've previously experienced.

The table is set

I met Jane (*not her real name*) few years ago on the train to Central London and we got on quite well, so we exchanged contacts. We hardly see each other but manage to grab coffee at one train station or another now and again and, most times I would pay the bill. Jane is an executive, she leads a busy life, makes great money but she often suffered from exhaustion, was disorganized and confused, ran late, and forgot things. Jane worked three times harder and longer than her colleagues, as a matter of fact, she prided herself on working long hours. She felt she needed to work more, sacrifice more to deserve her big salary and would always ask me "Aji how are you doing it? Where do you get money from?" When she got tired of keeping up appearances, she turned to me for help in a long email.

Do you know anyone like Jane?

Here is the thing, it seems many of us for too long have put our God idea on hold, relegating 'living' for a future time when we have accomplished all our goals. Our incessant drive to amass wealth, to be thought well of and mounting ever-new trophies on the walls of our life.

While you may have gained everything in the material sense, what if all these aren't part of the equation of your life? Just asking.

What would you do if everything that you have built and strived for and worked so hard to attain came tumbling down - I hear, "God forbid!"

But it happens and it doesn't matter - perhaps it's part of the equation.

What if what you're being taught in church is a fraction of the truth?

Just saying.

What if what you're praying for is what's working against you?

It was a delight working with Jane and seeing her transition from surviving to thriving. I'm always pleased reading all the wonderful things she's now doing with children. I shared some of the notes from other amazing women in the 'Notes' section of this book.

Just like Jane, I am now embracing what few years ago I would have considered one of the most dangerous games and I call it 'Graceful Living.' Would you like to join me? The table is set.

Here are 5 important steps to help you get started.

1. **Accept** that where you are right now, is where you ought to be at this moment in time.
2. **Develop** a deeper and unshakeable connection with your Inner Spirit – you can't get it through strategy or goal setting.

3. **Give yourself permission** to be vulnerable: this might mean taking risks, challenging the status quo, going on a journey, starting a new venture or even relocating geographically.

4. **Be Afraid** – Yes, be afraid and do it afraid! Figure out how you will deal with your fears, your insecurities, your excuses or any blocks that you will use to stop you or distract you from going on this journey. Get to know them and be ready to take action when they show up. If you are not focused, do not have self-belief or you are not really committed to the journey then you will give up.

5. **Live in the moment and be grateful**, make time to have fun and celebrate often. You will find that the more you do this the happier you will be and the closer you will be to making a living and having clarity around why you're here in the first instance!

It is not too late to embrace life. I know that you need to factor in the economics of earning money – however, you can make a living while making a life, people all over the world are doing it – So why can't you be one of these people?

Ambitious for His Will

In this adventurous life, I've come to realize that saying 'Yes' to the calling of God on our lives to live for more than just career and business success and comfort, to step outside of ourselves and live with an eternal perspective cannot be figured out. It cannot be taught in any business school or by any 'guru' – *it can only be achieved by a hungered and thirsty soul.*

I'm glad to let you know that, you are not called to carry out your day-to-day tasks in your own strength. You are not called to figure out how to best love people, I struggled with this for ages. You aren't even called to muster up a desire to bring God's kingdom to earth – trust me on this.

Look, all these weights rest on the shoulders of your heavenly Father. All that is required of you is to take time to let Him love you as you are, fill you with the desires of his heart, and follow his leadership into the fulfilment of those desires. Period!

God wants to take your five loaves of bread and two fish and multiply it to feed the souls of thousands. This can only be achieved when you and I say 'YES' to partnering with the Holy Spirit and allow God to use us to change the world by bringing His kingdom to earth through simple acts of love and obedience.

Doing God's will, will play out in some of the everyday decisions of marriage, parenting, work, friendship, and ministry. When you view your spouse as one of the gifts God has given you to help you choose and live wisely; when your work becomes a sacred place, people then become your most critical assets.

I hear people say often that they want to make a difference. You are making a difference everyday just being you, the you that God created with the joy and peace that can come only from Him. If people are seeing that in you, you are making a difference. They will know who to come to when they need encouragement and prayer. Keep that in mind as you go through your day. Walk through your life with purpose, knowing that you are **HIS LADY.**

So, each morning as you choose your clothing and your shoes, be aware of who you are; **HIS LADY**. Be intentional in your connections with people each day. Be led to wear the appropriate shoes, the appropriate attitude and purpose that will be what that person will need for that day.

Final word from Him

My boss (Yahweh) told me that you've prayed, have questions and been waiting on Him for answers. He said you're burdened with living out your purpose and how to navigate this life amidst the noise of societal expectations.

He's asked me to tell you that: Whenever you have a question, simply know that he's answered it already.

You only need to open your eyes to the world around you.

- His response could be in an article already published.
- In the sermon you heard yesterday or that is about to be delivered.
- In the movie, in the song you just listened to. In the words about to be spoken by someone close to you.
- Listen to His truth in the whisper of the wind, the babble of the brook, and the warmth of the sun.
- Listen to Him in the truth of your soul.
- Listen to Him in the feelings of your heart.
- Listen to Him in the quiet of your mind.
- Hear Him, everywhere.

For His truth is your surest help in time of need. Here is His promise: "I will never leave you nor forsake you!" – Hebrews 13:5 (NKJV)

Chapter 7

An Invitation

I s this you?

You have the know-how. You have a tiny idea of what your next level looks like. But something keeps coming up seemingly every day and preventing you from EXECUTING on the work for which you were created.

Because of this, you're sometimes depressed...

Not in the medical sense of the word; but you feel frustrated and bleak ....

My dear, if that's you, know this:

You've reached your tipping point and DESTINY is calling you!

Because it is IMPOSSIBLE for you to hold all the anointing the Lord deposited inside you without EXPLODING.

I have a feeling that there are decisions you wanted to make, but you haven't, and God is waiting for you to make them.

Trust me, it's time to pull out all the stops and make the sacrifices you must make.

The tools I provide in this book are just the beginning, however, there is so much more.

I'll like to invite you to join my 'MENTOR ME' PROGRAM.

The '**MENTOR ME' PROGRAM** is a declaration and total surrender to be mentored by Holy Spirit to take you through "The Tipping Point" – I am just the facilitator.

I'm here if you're ready to LET loose!

INTERESTED? programs@hislady.org

"WHY SETTLE WHEN YOU CAN SOAR "
– Aji R. Michael

LOVE NOTES

"Good afternoon, I got your mail a while back. Thank you for the swift reply

What can I say now am at a stagnant stage of my life, there are a bunch of stuff I want to do but I can't seem to put my mind and focus all my energy into them. Am first confused, then frustrated and top it all I can't feel my own myself, No enthusiasm to move on with life or take intentional steps to a better me... Am struggling"

"Awwwwww my BELOVED AJI..... I bless my stars that i met you! Thanks for this soul-bursting words.

I'm now enjoying my journey, knowing everyday is my Christmas, I'm not even eager about December 25th or any special day as Christmas...every blessed day is my Christmas!

I'm loving all the delays in my life because i just found out i needed them, I've grown past comparing my my beautiful small ass to anyone's.

Now my MOTTO goes thus: living the rich life as you said, living life non apologetically, ALIGNING and not hustling-I've just gotta understand ME, know my environment and know how i can be of HELP, that's better for me as

ALIGNMENT and not the word HUSTLE that somewhat means you have to sweat your life out to be close to happy.

I'm HAPPILY SINGLE, EXPLORING MY DEAR LIFE! Wish i can go on, mylove..(smiling)

I'm typing from my STREAM OF CONSCIOUSNESS! Just as it's flowing raw, from my beautiful soul.

I'm still working from my office, right now. I just had to reply you.

You mean a lot to me!

AJI TEMI NIKAN.

We still gotta talk more soon.

I ADORE YOU, Aji. #bighug"

"Dear Aji,

Thank you for yesterday's program......It was worth every time invested.

Well done! Thank you for following your heart, thank you for being overly ambitious because you are doing it for lots of us women out there.

Thank you for making a very rich and impacting program free.....I deeply appreciate this and do not take it for granted.

You are not alone in this journey.....we all are in it. Thank you for bringing me into the Savvy Women's Circle."

"Hello Aji,

Thank you so much.

I had a really good time too. I really learnt a lot, and also made some decisions yesterday.

A big congratulations to you, really.

Before attending this event, I always saw you as this glamorous woman who just wanted to put herself and her glamour out there, now I know you gunuinely care about the needs and concerns of other women and would do whatever it takes to see other women succeed, congratulations again.

Kudos also on the choice of speakers, Tosin and Mofoluwasola were very willing to share their contacts and assist further beyond the conference.

You are doing so much from your heart and God sees you and well, you know the rest.

Looking forward to seeing you again"

NOTES

Trait 1 BOLD

Courtney Joseph: 3 Lessons From Five Brave Women in the Book of Numbers, 2015; https://womenlivingwell.org

C. H. Mackintosh: **A Rightful Claim:** https://biblehub.com/sermons/auth/mackintosh/a_rightful_claim.htm

D. Young commentary on **The Disabilities Of Sex**: The Pulpit Commentary, Electronic Database. Accessed 25 June 2019

Wikipedia
In the Talmud and the Zohar the reference to Zelophehad having "died in his own sin" is used to equate him with the man executed for gathering sticks on the Sabbath, https://en.wikipedia.org/wiki/Daughters_of_Zelophehad

Trait 2: DESIRE

Charles C. Spurgeon, Sermons, Notes and Exposition: The Blessing of the High Priest https://www.sermonaudio.com/search.asp?speakeronly=true&currsection=sermonsspeaker&keyword=C._H._Spurgeon

Charles C. Spurgeon, Sermons, Notes and Exposition: Women's Rights -- a Parable
https://biblehub.com/sermons/auth/spurgeon/women%27s_rights_a_parable.htm

Trait 3: FAITH

RAY C. STEDMAN: Daring Daughters, 1964
https://www.raystedman.org/thematic-studies/characters-in-scripture/daring-daughters

Charles C. Spurgeon, Sermons, Notes and Exposition: Against Murmuring
https://www.preceptaustin.org/spurgeon_on_numbers

Michael, A. (2013). The Next Maverick: Ready To Shape The Future

Trait 4: PRAYER

Mark Batterson. (2012). The Circle Maker. Zondervan

Bible versions:

Please note that bible references in this book have been taken from the following versions:

- New King James Version (NKJV)
- New International Version (NIV)
- New Living Translation (NLT)
- English Standard Version (ESV)
- King James Version (KJV)
- Good News Translation (GNT)
- The Message (MSG)

(Please note that this list may not be exhaustive.)

Aji R. Michael is a master coach to highly successful women across the globe. Aji works at the intersection of ambition and grace to help women create the rich and fulfilling lives they desire. She is a mentor, guide, and cheerleader for a new generation.

Aji is on a mission to redefine living for the modern-day woman through her platform Hislady.org

HIS LADY

WWW.HISLADY.ORG

Let's be friends

RedefiningLiving

RedefiningLiving

RedefiningLV